D0662816

Encouraging
Thoughts
for
Women:
Comfort

© 2016 by Barbour Publishing, Inc.

Written and compiled by Shanna D. Gregor.

Print ISBN 978-1-63409-958-5

All rights reserved. No part of this publication may be reproduced or transmitted for commercial purposes, except for brief quotations in printed reviews, without written permission of the publisher.

Churches and other noncommercial interests may reproduce portions of this book without the express written permission of Barbour Publishing, provided that the text does not exceed 500 words or 5 percent of the entire book, whichever is less, and that the text is not material quoted from another publisher. When reproducing text from this book, include the following credit line: "From *Encouraging Thoughts for Women: Comfort*, published by Barbour Publishing, Inc. Used by permission."

Scripture quotations marked NIV are taken from the HOLY BIBLE, NEW INTERNATIONAL VERSION®. NIV®. Copyright © 1973, 1978, 1984, 2011 by Biblica, Inc.™ Used by permission. All rights reserved worldwide.

Scripture quotations marked ESV are taken from The Holy Bible, English Standard Version®, copyright © 2001 by Crossway Bibles, a publishing ministry of Good News Publishers. Used by permission. All rights reserved.

Scripture quotations marked NLT are taken from the *Holy Bible*. New Living Translation copyright© 1996, 2004, 2015 by Tyndale House Foundation. Used by permission of Tyndale House Publishers, Inc. Carol Stream, Illinois 60188. All rights reserved.

Scripture quotations marked NKJV are taken from the New King James Version®. Copyright © 1982 by Thomas Nelson, Inc. Used by permission. All rights reserved.

Scripture quotations marked NCV are taken from the New Century Version of the Bible, copyright © 2005 by Thomas Nelson, Inc. Used by permission. All rights reserved.

Published by Barbour Books, an imprint of Barbour Publishing, Inc., P.O. Box 719, Uhrichsville, Ohio 44683, www.barbourbooks.com

Our mission is to publish and distribute inspirational products offering exceptional value and biblical encouragement to the masses.

 Member of the
Evangelical Christian
Publishers Association

Printed in the United States of America.

Encouraging
Thoughts
for
Women:

Comfort

BARBOUR BOOKS
An Imprint of Barbour Publishing, Inc.

Contents

Introduction

We can all use some encouragement and a little comfort throughout the day. Every road in life presents some level of difficulty. We live in a fallen world where we all experience hurt, pain, loss, and disappointment on different levels—but there is hope. No matter where you are on your journey, no matter how difficult your journey seems at the time, you don't have to travel alone. God, your constant companion, promises to be there to comfort you every step of the way.

One encouraging word from Him or those He sets in your path can give you just what you need at the moment. May *Encouraging Thoughts for Women: Comfort* inspire you to trust God and allow Him to comfort you throughout your day.

Shanna D. Gregor

Perspective

Come Up Higher

And Moses said to the people, "Fear not,
stand firm, and see the salvation of the LORD,
which he will work for you today."

EXODUS 14:13 ESV

"Come on, Donna," her coworker, Angie, called as Donna
pulled her sweatshirt on over her T-shirt, locked her car,
and snapped her fanny pack around her waist.

How did I ever let her talk me into a hike? Donna
thought. *This is so not my thing.*

Donna knew she needed to get out of the house,
away from the stress of the financial difficulty she was
facing, but the challenge of an early morning, mountain
hike felt like too much.

About twenty minutes into the hike, Donna fell far
behind. Angie shouted down to her and said, "Come
up higher! There's so much more to see." She pressed
herself harder and caught up with her friend.

"Doesn't the path look different from this perspective?" Angie asked. Donna had been so consumed in thought about her problems, she'd completely ignored the beauty around her. She sat down on a rock and emotion overwhelmed her. She sensed God's presence. "Come up higher," He seemed to say to her. "Take a look from my perspective."

Angie noticed the tears in Donna's eyes. Donna smiled and said, "I have been shortsighted and allowed my negative circumstances to consume me. Thank you for reminding me to allow God to take me higher, where I must take the focus off of me and see God's path before me by faith."

*Look carefully then how you walk, not as
unwise but as wise, making the best use of the
time, because the days are evil. Therefore do
not be foolish, but understand what the will of the
Lord is. And do not get drunk with wine, for that
is debauchery, but be filled with the Spirit.*
EPHESIANS 5:15–18 ESV

---

*He [God] made known his ways to Moses,
his deeds to the people of Israel.*
PSALM 103:7 NIV

---

*Solid food is for those who are mature,
who through training have the skill to recognize
the difference between right and wrong.*
HEBREWS 5:14 NLT

"If we were to gain God's perspective,
even for a moment, and were to look at
the way we go through life accumulating
and hoarding and displaying our things,
we would have the same feelings of horror
and pity that any sane person has when he
views people in an asylum endlessly
beating their heads against the wall."

RANDY ALCORN

"Once we deeply trust that we ourselves
are precious in God's eyes, we are able to
recognize the preciousness of others and
their unique places in God's heart."

HENRI J. M. NOUWEN

"Faith is a way of looking at the
world from God's perspective."

RICK WARREN

A Clear Perspective

*"My thoughts are not your thoughts, neither
are your ways my ways," declares the LORD.
"As the heavens are higher than the earth,
so are my ways higher than your ways and
my thoughts than your thoughts."*

ISAIAH 55:8–9 NIV

"We plan, God laughs." While the saying gets a
chuckle, we're usually not chuckling when our plans
go awry. But step back and look at the situation
from another perspective—God's perspective. He
sees your future as clearly as He sees your past and
present, and He knows how to get you from here to
there. Ask the Holy Spirit to help you look from
God's perspective—and laugh with the joy of
knowing you remain under His watchful care!

God, when I focus on my problems, it's easy to take my eyes off You. I can grow shortsighted and even blind to Your truth. Help me to choose to come up higher today. Give me strength to take my focus off myself and see my life from Your perspective. I choose to live each day from Your viewpoint, focused on the purpose, and living the plan You've destined for me.

We do this by keeping our eyes on Jesus, the champion who initiates and perfects our faith. Because of the joy awaiting him, he endured the cross, disregarding its shame. Now he is seated in the place of honor beside God's throne.

HEBREWS 12:2 NLT

My brethren, count it all joy when you fall into various trials, knowing that the testing of your faith produces patience.

JAMES 1:2–3 NKJV

"The eye is the lamp of the body. So, if your eye is healthy, your whole body will be full of light."

MATTHEW 6:22 ESV

Heavenly Father, sometimes life presses in and it's difficult for me to lift my head. In those moments when my heart is heavy, whisper to me gently and remind me I belong to You. Give me a firm assurance that all things work together for my good. Call me to come up to the higher places and rest in You. When I rise with You above the difficulties of life, I find my confidence in You.

"Grant me, O Lord, to know what I ought to know, to love what I ought to love, to praise what delights you most, to value what is precious in your sight."

THOMAS À KEMPIS

"Choose to view life through God's eyes. This will not be easy because it doesn't come naturally to us. We cannot do this on our own. We have to allow God to elevate our vantage point. Start by reading His Word, the Bible. . . . Pray and ask God to transform your thinking. Let Him do what you cannot. Ask Him to give you an eternal, divine perspective."

CHARLES SWINDOLL

Questions

Question and Answer

Before they call I will answer;
while they are yet speaking I will hear.
ISAIAH 65:24 ESV

"Why, Mommy?" the tiny voice in the backseat of the car chirped for what felt like the umpteenth time. Amy exhaled rather loudly as she turned into the day-care parking lot. Her daughter Amanda's incessant desire for knowledge couldn't be quenched, or was it just a desire to keep an exchange going on and on? Whatever the case, Amy was already exhausted and it wasn't even 8 a.m.

Amy parked the car, gathered Amanda's things for the day, and gently lifted her out of her car seat, trying to remember the last question her daughter asked. Amanda's tiny hand slipped tightly around Amy's finger as they walked across the parking lot and into the school foyer.

She lingered a moment at the classroom door,

watching her daughter's exchange with another student before heading back to the car. During her commute she relished the silence as her thoughts turned to God. She usually spent her commute time in prayer. She knew God was there, listening. She believed He would always give her the answers she needed in His time.

Amy remembered the sparkle in her daughter's eyes and the excitement in her voice with each new question. It was a season of childhood she wanted to cherish. Soon her little one would be all grown up and on her own. "Help me to respond to her with Your patience and love," she prayed.

And without faith it is impossible to please him, for whoever would draw near to God must believe that he exists and that he rewards those who seek him.

HEBREWS 11:6 ESV

"Keep on asking, and you will receive what you ask for. Keep on seeking, and you will find. Keep on knocking, and the door will be opened to you. For everyone who asks, receives. Everyone who seeks, finds. And to everyone who knocks, the door will be opened."

MATTHEW 7:7–8 NLT

"For inquire, please, of the former age, and consider the things discovered by their fathers."

JOB 8:8 NKJV

"He wishes to give who advises us to ask."
AUGUSTINE

"Some people think God does not like to be troubled with our constant coming and asking. The way to trouble God is not to come at all."
DWIGHT L. MOODY

"A prudent question is one-half of wisdom."
FRANCIS BACON

"There are those who insist that it is a very bad thing to question God. To them, 'why?' is a rude question. That depends, I believe, on whether it is an honest search, in faith, for His meaning, or whether it is the challenge of unbelief and rebellion."
ELISABETH ELLIOT

Ask in Faith

On the day I called, you answered me;
my strength of soul you increased.
PSALM 138:3 ESV

"What is this?" "Where are we now?" "How come this is this way?" One thing children know how to do is ask questions. Mothers know, however, that their children might not be ready or able to hear the answers to all of their questions, so they answer the ones they can and tuck the others away. Your heavenly Father hears your questions, all of them. But He doesn't give you all the answers at once. Trust Him to know what you can handle.

Lord, I know I ask You a lot of questions, and You never tire of my voice. You never become frustrated or irritated at my constant inquisitions. Sometimes Your response doesn't make me feel any better, or I don't understand any more than I did before I asked, but thank You for listening. I know You are always listening. And I trust You to give me the answers I need in the perfect time I need them.

After three days they found him in the temple, sitting among the teachers, listening to them and asking them questions. And all who heard him were amazed at his understanding and his answers.

LUKE 2:46–47 ESV

If any of you lacks wisdom, you should ask God, who gives generously to all without finding fault, and it will be given to you.

JAMES 1:5 NIV

And this is the confidence that we have toward him, that if we ask anything according to his will he hears us.

1 JOHN 5:14 ESV

Let us then with confidence draw near to the throne of grace, that we may receive mercy and find grace to help in time of need.

HEBREWS 4:16 ESV

And we have received God's Spirit (not the world's spirit), so we can know the wonderful things God has freely given us.

1 CORINTHIANS 2:12 NLT

My heart has heard you say, "Come and talk with me." And my heart responds, "LORD, I am coming."

PSALM 27:8 NLT

Questions

"Call to me and I will answer you and tell you
great and unsearchable things you do not know."
JEREMIAH 33:3 NIV

If you have ever worked with children, you know
they will sometimes ask a question but not listen to
your answer. As God's child, avoid doing the same
thing. Pose your questions to God, and then listen
to His answer. You may not like what you hear—it
may be difficult to accept or sound unreasonable to
you. Ask the Holy Spirit to deepen your understanding and give you the power to accept even the
most difficult of God's unsearchable answers.

Father, I'm learning that in order to get the right answer, I should ask the right question. You know my heart, and You've set a path before me. Give me wisdom and insight to ask You the right questions that will lead me in the way You would have me go. Help me to accept the answers to the questions that are hard to hear. Give me a heart of obedience.

"Not until we have become humble and teachable, standing in awe of God's holiness and sovereignty. Acknowledging our own littleness, distrusting our own thoughts, and willing to have our minds turned upside down, can divine wisdom become ours."

J. I. PACKER

———————————————

"Hasty conclusions are the mark of a fool; a wise man doubteth; a fool rageth and is confident; the novice saith, 'I am sure that it is so'; the better learned answers, 'Peradventure, it may be so; but, I pray thee, inquire.'"

JEREMY TAYLOR

———————————————

"My prayers, my God, flow from what I am not; I think Thy answers make me what I am."

GEORGE MACDONALD

Wisdom

Comfort in His Wisdom

*Through wisdom a house is built, and by understanding
it is established; by knowledge the rooms are
filled with all precious and pleasant riches.*

PROVERBS 24:3–4 NKJV

Chelsea stepped out of their little camper they were
calling home while the last touches were being added to
their new house. She and her husband, Caleb, decided
to move home. They believed it would be the perfect
place to raise their own family, but there were very few
houses on the market in the small town, so they decided
to build one.

She carried a tall glass of iced tea over to Caleb
who was helping a crew apply the final touches to the
trim. "Ready for a break?" she asked.

Caleb smiled and pushed her hair away from her
face as he took the tea and chugged it down. "Ahh, that
was great. It wet my whistle," he teased.

"I'm so glad we decided to build this house," Chelsea commented. "There were so many decisions, so many challenges, and so many things we just didn't know."

Caleb nodded in agreement. "We made mistakes, and it cost us a little to learn things, but the biggest lesson I think we learned is that God is our wisdom. We can rely on Him for every decision in our lives—big or small."

Chelsea took the empty tea glass out of his hand as he picked up the paintbrush. "And when we do make mistakes, He comforts us and shows us a way out. I'm so thankful for that."

Wisdom

Joyful is the person who finds wisdom,
the one who gains understanding.
For wisdom is more profitable than silver,
and her wages are better than gold.
Wisdom is more precious than rubies;
nothing you desire can compare with her.
She offers you long life in her right hand,
and riches and honor in her left.
She will guide you down delightful paths;
all her ways are satisfying.
Wisdom is a tree of life to those who embrace her;
happy are those who hold her tightly.

PROVERBS 3:13–18 NLT

"Wisdom is the ability to use knowledge so as to meet successfully the emergencies of life. Men may acquire knowledge, but wisdom is a gift direct from God."
BOB JONES

"I must not depend on anything that I could do, but to look to Him for strength and wisdom."
MARIA WOODWORTH-ETTER

"If you young fellows were wise, the devil couldn't do anything to you, but since you aren't wise, you need us who are old."
MARTIN LUTHER

Wisdom Is Life

Wisdom is a tree of life to those who embrace her;
happy are those who hold her tightly.

PROVERBS 3:18 NLT

Perhaps you thought you had a great idea, but it turned out to be a big mistake. You wish you had listened to warnings and given the matter more thought. Let God use this teachable moment to give you the gift of wisdom. The wisdom from above may seem counterintuitive at times, but you can be certain it won't fail you. It is embedded in the timeless nature of God, who sees from eternity to eternity.

Heavenly Father, thank You for comforting me and loving me unconditionally when I refused to follow wisdom. You have made all wisdom available to me. I don't want to do things my way. I choose Your path for my life. Speak Your wisdom to my heart. Show me how to follow You in all things. Open my ears to hear You speaking, and teach me Your ways. I'm listening.

*But the wisdom from above is first pure,
then peaceable, gentle, open to reason, full of
mercy and good fruits, impartial and sincere.*
JAMES 3:17 ESV

---

*Intelligent people are always ready to learn.
Their ears are open for knowledge.*
PROVERBS 18:15 NLT

---

*Let the word of Christ dwell in you richly in all
wisdom, teaching and admonishing one another
in psalms and hymns and spiritual songs,
singing with grace in your hearts to the Lord.*
COLOSSIANS 3:16 NKJV

---

*Reflect on what I am saying, for the
Lord will give you insight into all this.*
2 TIMOTHY 2:7 NIV

*Yet among the mature we do impart wisdom,
although it is not a wisdom of this age or of the
rulers of this age, who are doomed to pass away.
But we impart a secret and hidden wisdom of God,
which God decreed before the ages for our glory.
None of the rulers of this age understood this, for if
they had, they would not have crucified the Lord of
glory. But, as it is written, "What no eye has seen,
nor ear heard, nor the heart of man imagined,
what God has prepared for those who love him."*

1 CORINTHIANS 2:6–9 ESV

Godly Wisdom

If any of you lacks wisdom, let him ask of God,
who gives to all liberally and without reproach,
and it will be given to him.

JAMES 1:5 NKJV

Wisdom seems like such a lofty goal, yet it's what God offers to you freely and generously, simply for the asking. You see, His wisdom has nothing to do with graduate degrees but everything to do with a humble willingness to sit in the school of the Holy Spirit. Open His Word and learn from it. Meditate on its meaning and apply it to your heart and your life. This is genuine wisdom.

Thank You, Lord, for Your divine wisdom. It comforts me knowing that You perfect everything that concerns me. You have given me Your very best. It can be overwhelming to endure hardship, but that is when I feel closest to You. No matter what I'm facing, Your wisdom is at work on my behalf. I trust You to bring good out of difficulty, joy out of sorrow, and peace out of pain.

"Every morning, read seriously and reverently a portion of the Holy Scriptures, and acquaint yourselves with the history and doctrine thereof. It is a book full of light and wisdom, will make you wise to eternal life, and furnish you with directions and principles to guide and order your life safely and prudently."

MATTHEW HALE

"Common sense suits itself to the ways of the world. Wisdom tries to conform to the ways of Heaven."

JOSEPH JOUBERT

"We seem to gain wisdom more readily through our failures than through our successes. We always think of failure as the antithesis of success, but it isn't. Success often lies just the other side of failure."

LEO BUSCAGLIA

Motives

Intentions of the Heart

For we speak as messengers approved by
God to be entrusted with the Good News.
Our purpose is to please God, not people.
He alone examines the motives of our hearts.

1 Thessalonians 2:4 NLT

Holly slammed the dishwasher with a lot more force than she intended. Her husband, Jake, noticed her frustration. "Okay, spill," he challenged. "You've not been yourself all night."

"I did something at work today and I shouldn't have. I took an idea a team member shared with me, built on it a little, and presented it to leadership as my own idea."

Jake's shock and disbelief was evident.

"I know it was awful of me," she said between sobs. "I shouldn't have done it, but I justified it as 'managing' my career just like everybody else does."

Jake's voice was soft. "We're not everybody. Our motives shouldn't be the same as others. We do what we do to please Christ."

His words cut like a knife. Tears of regret streamed down her face. "I need to check my heart. Am I hurting because I hurt a coworker, or because I have to endure the consequences of my actions? I've deceived myself into believing it would all be okay. And it won't."

Jake took her hand. "You love God above all else, and He loves you. He'll help you keep your heart right and your motives pure when you stay in close relationship with Him. Come on. Let's go to Him in prayer about this, together."

Make allowance for each other's faults, and forgive anyone who offends you. Remember, the Lord forgave you, so you must forgive others.

COLOSSIANS 3:13 NLT

For where your treasure is, there your heart will be also.

LUKE 12:34 NKJV

Do not be conformed to this world, but be transformed by the renewal of your mind, that by testing you may discern what is the will of God, what is good and acceptable and perfect.

ROMANS 12:2 ESV

As in water face reflects face, so a man's heart reveals the man.

PROVERBS 27:19 NKJV

"Repentance removes old sins and wrong attitudes,
and it opens the way for the Holy Spirit
to restore our spiritual health."
SHIRLEY DOBSON

"Nothing can be great which is not right. Nothing
which reason condemns can be suitable to the
dignity of the human mind. To be driven by external
motives from the path which our heart approves,
to give way to anything but conviction, to suffer
the opinion of others to rule our choice or overpower
our resolves, is to submit tamely to the lowest
and most ignominious slavery, and to resign the
right of directing our own lives."
SAMUEL JOHNSON

Selfless Motives

*Serve him with wholehearted devotion and with
a willing mind, for the LORD searches every heart and
understands every desire and every thought.*

1 CHRONICLES 28:9 NIV

We claim publicly we're asking for no reward but
seek acclaim privately when no reward comes our
way. If you find yourself harboring offense, check
the motives behind your charitable acts. God
already has. Ask Him to replace selfish motives
with selfless ones and to instill in you a spirit of
compassion, kindness, and generosity. On the
outside, you'll continue doing the good things
you've been doing. On the inside, you'll be doing
them for the right reason.

Father, You know the motivations of my heart. Even if no one knows or would ever find out something I consider doing, You know it and I want—more than anything—to please You. Forgive me for my selfishness. Give me grace and peace to trust that You will perfect all things that concern me. I trust You for the outcome, and I refuse to manipulate or try to control the outcome.

But the LORD said to Samuel, "Do not look at his appearance or at his physical stature, because I have refused him. For the LORD does not see as man sees; for man looks at the outward appearance, but the LORD looks at the heart."

1 SAMUEL 16:7 NKJV

For the word of God is alive and active. Sharper than any double-edged sword, it penetrates even to dividing soul and spirit, joints and marrow; it judges the thoughts and attitudes of the heart.

HEBREWS 4:12 NIV

The LORD saw that the human beings on the earth
were very wicked and that everything they thought
about was evil. He was sorry he had made human
beings on the earth, and his heart was filled with pain.

GENESIS 6:5–6 NCV

And no creature is hidden from his sight,
but all are naked and exposed to the eyes
of him to whom we must give account.

HEBREWS 4:13 ESV

The heart is deceitful above all things,
and desperately sick; who can understand it?

JEREMIAH 17:9 ESV

Motives of Others

Pursue righteousness, faith, love and peace, along with those who call on the Lord out of a pure heart.

2 TIMOTHY 2:22 NIV

———————————

Though your motives are pure toward others, you will encounter those whose hearts aren't pure, and it hurts to find out someone has used you for their own purposes. When that happens—and it almost certainly will at one time or another—take comfort in God. You can be sure that even when others are untrue, God never wavers. He is always thinking of you, putting your best interests first.

Lord, open my eyes to the intents and motives of the hearts of others when it concerns me. Give me a discerning heart to see when someone desires to hurt me or use me for their own purposes. Give me a love that can only come from You to forgive them. Give me a desire to truly see Your good come from a difficult situation, and comfort me so that I may rise above the pain.

"God made man to go by motives, and He will not go without them, any more than a boat without steam or a balloon without gas."
HENRY WARD BEECHER

—————————

"If virtue accompanies beauty it is the heart's paradise; if vice be associated with it, it is the soul's purgatory. It is the wise man's bonfire, and the fool's furnace."
FRANCIS QUARLES

—————————

"God sees hearts and we see faces."
GEORGE HERBERT

—————————

"None but God can satisfy the longing of the immortal soul; as the heart was made for Him, He only can fill it."
RICHARD TRENCH

Dreams

A Heart Set on Something Higher

"My grace is sufficient for you, for my power is made perfect in weakness." Therefore I will boast all the more gladly of my weaknesses, so that the power of Christ may rest upon me. For the sake of Christ, then, I am content with weaknesses, insults, hardships, persecutions, and calamities. For when I am weak, then I am strong.

2 Corinthians 12:8–10 esv

Peyton longed for a home. The many moves she made to support her husband, Donnie's career advancements often led them to rent a house, or if they purchased a house, it seldom meant more than a few years in that home. Once again, far from family and friends, she found herself sitting in a rental house surrounded by empty walls—empty because she didn't have the desire to put anything on them.

"Lord, why do I dream of a beautifully designed home with pictures of my family on the walls if it's something I'll really never have?" she asked often. On this particular morning, she especially missed that place she could call "home."

Suddenly she felt for sure that the Lord was with her. He spoke to her heart and let her know how much He loved her. She felt His assurance that her dreams were important to Him. Then He impressed upon her to set her heart on Him—to make Him her one desire above all else. His presence comforted her, and she knew He was really all she needed.

"For the Lord GOD does nothing without revealing his secret to his servants the prophets."

AMOS 3:7 ESV

Now faith is the assurance of things hoped for, the conviction of things not seen.

HEBREWS 11:1 ESV

But the anointing that you received from him abides in you, and you have no need that anyone should teach you. But as his anointing teaches you about everything, and is true, and is no lie— just as it has taught you, abide in him.

1 JOHN 2:27 ESV

*"Obstacles are those frightful things you
see when you take your eyes off the goal."*
HANNAH MORE

"The goal of a virtuous life is to become like God."
GREGORY OF NYSSA

---

*"God has never ceased to be the one
true aim of all right human aspirations."*
ALEXANDRE VINET

---

*"The first priority of my life is to be holy,
and the second goal of my life is to be a scholar."*
JOHN WESLEY

Let Him Be Your Dream Come True

*For God is working in you, giving you the desire
and the power to do what pleases him.*

PHILIPPIANS 2:13 NLT

When "no" evicts your cherished hopes and dreams,
bitterness often moves in—and stays. Avoid the
temptation to let disappointment replace your
dreams, and instead let God's Spirit find a home in
your heart. Tell Him your dreams, then listen for His
answer. Discover His "yes" in the blessings around
you, in your abilities and opportunities, and in the
work He has given you to do. Let following Him be
your dream come true!

Lord, I have many dreams, some more significant than others. I have no doubt many of them were placed in my heart by You. Lord, give me a desire above all else to look to You and wait patiently for those dreams You have for me. Forgive me when I try to make things happen on my own. I trust You for them to be realized at just the right time.

*But we urge you, brethren, that you increase
more and more; that you also aspire to lead a
quiet life, to mind your own business, and to work
with your own hands, as we commanded you,
that you may walk properly toward those who
are outside, and that you may lack nothing.*

1 THESSALONIANS 4:10–12 NKJV

---

*It is for freedom that Christ has set us free.
Stand firm, then, and do not let yourselves
be burdened again by a yoke of slavery.*

GALATIANS 5:1 NIV

---

*So whether you eat or drink, or whatever you do,
do it all for the glory of God.*

1 CORINTHIANS 10:31 NLT

*Now to him who is able to do immeasurably
more than all we ask or imagine, according to
his power that is at work within us.*
EPHESIANS 3:20 NIV

---

*You are from God and have overcome them, for he
who is in you is greater than he who is in the world.*
1 JOHN 4:4 ESV

---

*We are pressed on every side by troubles,
but we are not crushed. We are perplexed,
but not driven to despair.*
2 CORINTHIANS 4:8 NLT

---

*Be diligent to present yourself approved to God,
a worker who does not need to be ashamed,
rightly dividing the word of truth.*
2 TIMOTHY 2:15 NKJV

Aspirations from Him

Not that I have already attained, or am already
perfected; but I press on, that I may lay hold of
that for which Christ Jesus has also laid hold of me.
PHILIPPIANS 3:12 NKJV

Are you driven by that little voice inside you that
keeps telling you to reach higher, try harder, and
never give up until you attain a certain goal in your
life? If your goal is within the scope of God's will,
that voice is almost certainly His. It isn't His will for
you to seek out temporal things like money, fame,
or possessions. But He does want you to aspire to
become everything He has created you to be.

Heavenly Father, You steady my heart. When disappointment overshadows me and I'm consumed with unmet expectations, You comfort me. Forgive me for holding tight to things that really aren't from You. Help me to focus on the path You've set before me. Help me to process my pain in a way that brings You honor. Thank You for holding me through it all.

"The God who created, names and numbers the stars in the heavens also numbers the hairs of my head. He pays attention to very big things and to very small ones. What matters to me matters to Him, and that changes my life."
ELISABETH ELLIOTT

"Far away there in the sunshine are my highest aspirations. I may not reach them, but I can look up and see their beauty, believe in them, and try to follow where they lead."
LOUISA MAY ALCOTT

Forgiveness

Forgiveness—
A Matter of Heart

Do not repay evil for evil or reviling for reviling,
but on the contrary, bless, for to this you
were called, that you may obtain a blessing.
1 PETER 3:9 ESV

Kassie watched her adult son pick at his meal. She didn't get to see him very often since he rented an apartment on the south side of town, forty-five minutes opposite of the home he grew up in. He worked six days a week, often twelve-hour days.

He broke the silence, "Mom, I know what you're going to say, and I can't forgive her."

Her heart broke for him. She hated watching him navigate the hurt of another breakup with his on-again, off-again girlfriend. "You don't have to," she said. Sam looked up at her, and she continued: "At least not on your own. Forgiveness contains the word, *give*. When you choose to give—even when you don't feel you can—through faith, God will help you do it. It's His ability working through you that will empower you to give a gift to her—and to yourself."

Sam was listening.

"The gift of forgiveness allows you to live a grudge-free life. As you let go of the anger and pain, something wonderful happens—the Comforter comes in and begins to do a work in your heart."

His eyes filled with tears. "I want that, Mom. I do. Will you pray for me to be able to do that?"

Kassie reached across the table and took his hands in hers. "Let's pray now."

*"For if you forgive men their trespasses,
your heavenly Father will also forgive you.
But if you do not forgive men their trespasses,
neither will your Father forgive your trespasses."*

MATTHEW 6:14–15 NKJV

---

*We have this hope as an anchor for the soul,
firm and secure. It enters the inner sanctuary
behind the curtain, where our forerunner, Jesus,
has entered on our behalf. He has become a high
priest forever, in the order of Melchizedek.*

HEBREWS 6:19–20 NIV

---

*O Lord, you are so good, so ready to forgive, so full
of unfailing love for all who ask for your help.*

PSALM 86:5 NLT

Jesus, You looked down from the cross and asked God the Father to forgive those who put You there. Thank You for that example of forgiveness. You know what it feels like to be wrongly accused and betrayed. Thank You for giving me what I need to forgive those who hurt me. Help me to let it go, so that I can begin to heal. Thank You for walking through this with me.

*He will not constantly accuse us, nor remain
angry forever. He does not punish us for all
our sins; he does not deal harshly with us,
as we deserve. For his unfailing love toward
those who fear him is as great as the height of
the heavens above the earth. He has removed our
sins as far from us as the east is from the west.*

PSALM 103:9–12 NLT

---

*"And whenever you stand praying, forgive,
if you have anything against anyone,
so that your Father also who is in heaven
may forgive you your trespasses."*

MARK 11:25 ESV

"If I am walking along the street with a very disfiguring hole in the back of my dress, of which I am in ignorance, it is certainly a very great comfort to me to have a kind friend who will tell me of it. And similarly it is indeed a comfort to know that there is always abiding with me a divine, all-seeing Comforter, who will reprove me for all my faults, and will not let me go on in a fatal unconsciousness of them."

HANNAH WHITALL SMITH

The First to Forgive

*Make allowance for each other's faults,
and forgive anyone who offends you. Remember,
the Lord forgave you, so you must forgive others.*
COLOSSIANS 3:13 NLT

No one wants to be the first to say "I'm sorry." No one jumps to take responsibility for a misspoken word, a hurtful act, a mismanaged situation. But without someone possessing the humble courage to extend the hand of peace, no healing can ever take place. Do your part by stepping forward, admitting your part, and asking forgiveness of anyone you may have offended. Jesus forgave you first. True heart healing begins with your willingness to be first in the same way.

Jesus, I need forgiveness. I know You've forgiven me, but help me to have the courage to swallow my pride and ask those I've hurt for forgiveness. And if they are unwilling to forgive me, help me to process their decision right. Forgiveness is a choice. Thank You for Your unconditional love. Give me the words I need to truly speak to their heart and help them heal.

But if we confess our sins to him,
he is faithful and just to forgive us our sins
and to cleanse us from all wickedness.
1 John 1:9 nlt

───────────────

"I, even I, am He who blots out your
transgressions for My own sake;
and I will not remember your sins."
Isaiah 43:25 nkjv

───────────────

"Come now, let us settle the matter," says
the Lord. "Though your sins are like scarlet,
they shall be as white as snow; though they
are red as crimson, they shall be like wool."
Isaiah 1:18 niv

───────────────

As far as the east is from the west, so far
does he remove our transgressions from us.
Psalm 103:12 esv

"He that cannot forgive others, breaks the bridge over which he himself must pass if he would ever reach heaven; for everyone has need to be forgiven."
GEORGE HERBERT

"Did I offer peace today? Did I bring a smile to someone's face? Did I say words of healing? Did I let go of my anger and resentment? Did I forgive? Did I love? These are the real questions. I must trust that the little bit of love that I sow now will bear many fruits, here in this world and the life to come."
HENRI NOUWEN

Betrayal

He will shelter you with his wings. His faithful
promises are your armor and protection.
PSALM 91:4 NLT

Betrayal is such a bitter word. It's always personal.
You invested yourself in someone and that person
purposefully turned away. Whenever you place your
trust in a human being, you risk betrayal. We just
don't have the wherewithal to remain 100 percent
faithful. But God does. And He promises never
to betray the trust you place in Him. He'll even be
there to pick up the pieces, to comfort you, when
others fail you.

Lord, after betrayal, I want to close off my heart to everyone who could potentially hurt me. I don't want to feel this way. I want to have an open heart, ready to love others. I trust You to hold me tight while I heal. I open up to You and allow Your promises to mend me. I want to keep my heart pliable to You. Give me Your strength to trust others again.

*"To love means loving the unlovable.
To forgive means pardoning the unpardonable.
Faith means believing the unbelievable. Hope
means hoping when everything seems hopeless."*
Gilbert K. Chesterton

---

*"We must develop and maintain the capacity
to forgive. He who is devoid of the power to
forgive is devoid of the power to love. There
is some good in the worst of us and some evil
in the best of us. When we discover this,
we are less prone to hate our enemies."*
Martin Luther King Jr.

Patience

Peace through Patience

Strengthened with all might, according to His glorious power, for all patience and longsuffering with joy; giving thanks to the Father who has qualified us to be partakers of the inheritance of the saints in the light.

COLOSSIANS 1:11–12 NKJV

Sarah watched her friend, Beth, fidget in the checkout line. "Ugh, why don't they ever have enough checkers?" Beth exclaimed. "I don't have any patience. It's impossible for me to be still."

Sarah pushed the shopping cart forward in the line. "Beth, patience benefits you, others around you, and is vital in your relationship with God. But it takes work—for all of us."

"It certainly comes natural for you," Beth replied.

"Patience isn't natural for any of us. I have to work at it, too, and I need God's help. Waiting here in line, I try to understand my situation. I think about how most people treat the checkers. It's not their fault we're frustrated about the long lines. I try to be kind, helpful, and considerate to them, since most people aren't. Sometimes people ignore them, like they're invisible. As I practice patience in moments like this, it helps me wait on God in my relationship with Him."

Beth smiled. "I need patience. I know being still is important to hearing from Him. I want to learn to be patient. I want the peace that comes in waiting that you've demonstrated today."

But as for me, I watch in hope for the LORD,
I wait for God my Savior; my God will hear me.

MICAH 7:7 NIV

They who wait for the LORD shall renew their
strength; they shall mount up with wings like
eagles; they shall run and not be weary;
they shall walk and not faint.

ISAIAH 40:31 ESV

Now may the Lord direct your hearts into the
love of God and into the patience of Christ.

2 THESSALONIANS 3:5 NKJV

Lord, You know how hard waiting is for me. I used to be afraid to pray for patience, but I see now that patience will bring me into closer relationships—with You and with others. Teach me how to view things from another's perceptive. Help me to see whatever situation I'm facing from Your eyes. Give me understanding and compassion for others as I wait.

O LORD, in the morning you hear my voice; in the morning I prepare a sacrifice for you and watch.

PSALM 5:3 ESV

But if we look forward to something we don't yet have, we must wait patiently and confidently. And the Holy Spirit helps us in our weakness. For example, we don't know what God wants us to pray for. But the Holy Spirit prays for us with groanings that cannot be expressed in words. And the Father who knows all hearts knows what the Spirit is saying, for the Spirit pleads for us believers in harmony with God's own will.

ROMANS 8:25–27 NLT

*"Be patient with everyone,
but above all, with yourself."*
SAINT FRANCIS DE SALES

---

*"Let us be silent, that we may
hear the whisper of God."*
RALPH WALDO EMERSON

---

*"I think Christians fail so often to get answers to
their prayers because they do not wait long enough
on God. They just drop down and say a few words,
and then jump up and forget it and expect God
to answer them. Such praying always reminds me
of the small boy ringing his neighbor's door-bell,
and then running away as fast as he can go."*
E. M. BOUNDS

Take Comfort in God's Timetable

Let us not become weary in doing good,
for at the proper time we will reap
a harvest if we do not give up.

GALATIANS 6:9 NIV

Things aren't happening quickly enough, and
you're feeling frustrated. Pause for a moment and
compare your timetable with God's timetable. Evi-
dently they don't match! Instead of fighting against
His gracious will, put your trust in it. Let Him unfold
the hours, days, and years to you in His own time.
His time is, without fail, the right time. Learn from
Him the difference godly patience can work in your
heart, mind, and spirit.

Heavenly Father, I want to let patience have her perfect work, but it's so hard. Teach me how to quiet my mind while I wait on You. Give me strength to not get ahead of You, but instead wait on You to take the lead. Help me to realize that sometimes doing nothing is actually the best thing I can do in the situation before me. I trust You and wait on You today.

And He said, "My Presence will go with you,
and I will give you rest."
EXODUS 33:14 NKJV

So be strong and courageous,
all you who put your hope in the LORD!
PSALM 31:24 NLT

Let perseverance finish its work so that you may
be mature and complete, not lacking anything.
JAMES 1:4 NIV

Love is patient, love is kind. It does not envy,
it does not boast, it is not proud. It does not
dishonor others, it is not self-seeking, it is not
easily angered, it keeps no record of wrongs.
1 CORINTHIANS 13:4–5 NIV

"A blessed spirit is a mould ever more and more patient of the bright metal poured into it, a body ever more completely uncovered to the meridian blaze of the spiritual sun."

C. S. LEWIS

"Through the dark and stormy night
Faith beholds a feeble light
Up the blackness streaking;
Knowing God's own time is best,
In a patient hope I rest
For the full day-breaking!"

JOHN GREENLEAF WHITTIER

"Wait for the Lord. Behave yourself manfully, and be of good courage. Do not be faithless, but stay in your place and do not turn back."

THOMAS À KEMPIS

Patient While Walking with God

*He who is slow to anger is better than the mighty,
and he who rules his spirit than he who takes a city.*

PROVERBS 16:32 NKJV

"I'm not a patient person!" You've heard it said, and perhaps you've even said it yourself. Unfortunately, the statement supports a false idea about patience. Rather than an inborn personality trait given only to some, patience is a gift of the Holy Spirit worked in the hearts of those who love Him. Godly patience allows you to respond to life's trying situations with serenity and self-control, sure evidence of your continuing walk with God.

God, I am tired of jumping in and then wishing I hadn't. As Your child, it's not up to me to make things happen. I can trust You to bring things around to me in Your time. Forgive me for my quick response and short temper. Calm me with Your presence, and show me how to reflect Your heart to those around me with Your patience.

*"Nothing great is ever achieved
without much enduring."*
CATHERINE OF SIENA

---

*"Fall on your knees and grow there. There is
no burden of the spirit but is lighter by kneeling
under it. Prayer means not always talking to Him,
but waiting before Him till the dust settles
and the stream runs clear."*
F. B. MEYER

---

*"Our patience is demonstrated most
clearly when we settle ourselves and
focus on what we can do while we wait."*
CRYSTAL MCDOWELL

Surrender

Surrender through Trust in God

My son, give me your heart,
and let your eyes observe my ways.
PROVERBS 23:26 NKJV

Jesus must have been devastated as He faced the biggest battle of His earthly life. His disciples deserted Him, and His friends forgot Him. He asked His closest companions to pray with Him, yet He found them sleeping instead. Judas betrayed Him, and Peter denied Him.

There was no one to rely on—no one but God. Jesus knew the Father and trusted Him. Even when the Father looked away, Jesus cried out to Him. He laid His life down in faith, trusting fully in the Father's plan. He surrendered completely, and trusted God to see Him through death, burial, and resurrection. His immovable confidence held fast to God alone.

God knew you before He formed you in your mother's womb. There is never a moment that you are not in His thoughts. From the very beginning of time, your heavenly Father's love for you compelled Him to send His Son, Jesus, to the cross, so that through His death, burial, and resurrection, you could have an eternal relationship with Him.

When you feel like no one is there for you—remember God has not forgotten you. You can let go with confidence and surrender completely to Him.

*By his divine power, God has given us everything
we need for living a godly life. We have received
all of this by coming to know him, the one
who called us to himself by means of his
marvelous glory and excellence.*

2 PETER 1:3 NLT

---

*And going a little farther, [Jesus] fell on the ground
and prayed that, if it were possible, the hour might
pass from him. And he said, "Abba, Father, all things
are possible for you. Remove this cup from me.
Yet not what I will, but what you will."*

MARK 14:35–36 ESV

Lord, sometimes I forget that I don't have to make things happen. I forget that it's not up to me. I don't have to control the outcome. I choose today to surrender everything to You. You have promised to perfect everything that concerns me—so I trust You to do that. It may not look like I imagined, but I believe Your way is best. Help me to let go and surrender it all to You today.

Then Peter spoke up, "We have
left everything to follow you!"
MARK 10:28 NIV

─────────────────

"Yet if you devote your heart to him and stretch
out your hands to him, if you put away the sin
that is in your hand and allow no evil to dwell in
your tent, then, free of fault, you will lift up your
face; you will stand firm and without fear."
JOB 11:13–15 NIV

─────────────────

And he said to him, "You shall love the
Lord your God with all your heart and
with all your soul and with all your mind.
MATTHEW 22:37 ESV

"Whatever the particular call is, the particular sacrifice God asks you to make, the particular cross He wishes you to embrace, whatever the particular path He wants you to tread, will you rise up, and say in your heart, "Yes, Lord, I accept it; I submit, I yield, I pledge myself to walk in that path, and to follow that Voice, and to trust Thee with the consequences"? Oh! but you say, "I don't know what He will want next." No, we none of us know that, but we know we shall be safe in His hands."

CATHERINE BOOTH

Surrendering Yourself to God

*[Jesus said,] "If you try to hang on to your life,
you will lose it. But if you give up your life for my sake
and for the sake of the Good News, you will save it."*

MARK 8:35 NLT

You may have thought about the concept of
surrendering yourself to God, but you've hesitated
because you want to be who you are—not someone
else's puppet. Don't worry! After all, God is the one
who created you to be the unique woman you are.
He has no intention of tampering with that. His goal
is just to offer stability in your emotions and thought
life and to enhance your talents and abilities.
Surrender to the hand of God means fulfillment of
your deepest God-given desires.

I did it again, Father—I picked up something I'd given to You and took it on as my responsibility. I really meant it when I said You could have it. I really wanted to let go. I surrender it all to You now. I leave it at the altar, and walk away. When the care of it crosses my mind, remind me that I don't have to carry it anymore. I gave it to You.

*My old self has been crucified with Christ.
It is no longer I who live, but Christ lives in me.
So I live in this earthly body by trusting in the Son
of God, who loved me and gave himself for me.*
GALATIANS 2:20 NLT

---

*And whatever you do, do it heartily,
as to the Lord and not to men.*
COLOSSIANS 3:23 NKJV

---

*Through Christ you have come to trust in
God. And you have placed your faith and
hope in God because he raised Christ
from the dead and gave him great glory.*
1 PETER 1:21 NLT

"When you come back to God for pardon and salvation, come with all you have to lay all at His feet. Come with your body, to offer it as a living sacrifice upon His altar. Come with your soul and all its powers, and yield them in willing consecration to your God and Saviour. Come, bring them all along—everything, body, soul, intellect, imagination, acquirements—all, without reserve."

CHARLES FINNEY

"I surrendered unto Him all there was of me; everything! Then for the first time I realized what it meant to have real power."

KATHRYN KUHLMAN

Blessed is the man who makes the LORD
his trust, who does not turn to the proud,
to those who go astray after a lie!

PSALM 40:4 ESV

You will keep in perfect peace all who trust in you,
all whose thoughts are fixed on you! Trust in the
LORD *always, for the* LORD GOD *is the eternal Rock.*

ISAIAH 26:3–4 NLT

He saved us, not because of works done by
us in righteousness, but according to his
own mercy, by the washing of regeneration
and renewal of the Holy Spirit.

TITUS 3:5 ESV

Gratitude

Comfort through Thanksgiving

We can rejoice, too, when we run into problems and trials, for we know that they help us develop endurance. And endurance develops strength of character, and character strengthens our confident hope of salvation.

ROMANS 5:3–4 NLT

Ellie waved good-bye to her mother, Krista, as she backed out of the driveway. Wet, hot tears trickled down her face. She didn't know how soon she'd see her again. Krista had spent the last seven years living with Ellie and her family. Together they watched each of Ellie's three children leave the nest, and now Krista set out on a new adventure. She was moving in with Ellie's sister, who had just lost her husband, to help her with Ellie's niece and nephews who were still in elementary school.

She walked back into the house. Suddenly, the house felt cold and empty, and Ellie felt very alone. She clicked on the television and turned up the volume of the channel that played Christian music. She wanted to cry hard and feel sorry for herself, but she really couldn't. Instead of sorrow, her heart filled with gratitude as she recounted the many wonderful things she experienced with her mother.

She lifted her voice and her heart in praise and thanksgiving. God had allowed her to have her mother in her home for a long season. Their bond was strong. She rejoiced as she remembered the many moments they shared—memories she'd treasure forever. She felt her spirit lift as she continued to thank God for comforting her.

Let your roots grow down into him, and let
your lives be built on him. Then your faith
will grow strong in the truth you were taught,
and you will overflow with thankfulness.

COLOSSIANS 2:7 NLT

This is the day the LORD has made.
We will rejoice and be glad in it.

PSALM 118:24 NLT

But thanks be to God, who gives us the
victory through our Lord Jesus Christ.

1 CORINTHIANS 15:57 NKJV

Rejoice always, pray without ceasing,
give thanks in all circumstances; for this
is the will of God in Christ Jesus for you.

1 THESSALONIANS 5:16–18 ESV

"God understands His own plan, and He knows what you want a great deal better than you do. The very things that you most deprecate, as fatal limitations or obstructions, are probably what you most want. What you call hindrances, obstacles, discouragements, are probably God's opportunities. Bring down your soul, or rather, bring it up to receive God's will and do His work, in your lot, in your sphere, under your cloud of obscurity, against your temptations, and then you shall find that your condition is never opposed to your good, but really consistent with it."

HORACE BUSHNELL

God Is with You

Be thankful in all circumstances.
1 Thessalonians 5:18 nlt

If you are going through a difficult time in your life, your prayers may sound more like a list of woes than a song of thanksgiving. God wants you to bring to Him your cries of pain, but He also invites you to offer Him your thanks for the good things happening in your life. This is how He reminds you that you and the situation you're facing remain in His hands. Be thankful, because God is present with you—loving and comforting you—every moment of every day.

Father, I am so thankful for the good things You've placed in my life. I am thankful for the friends and family—the people who speak into my life and lift me up. No matter what I face, no matter how I feel, I can always find something to be grateful for—my life, my health, my relationship with You. Thank You for who You are and who You created me to be.

That I may proclaim with the voice of thanksgiving,
and tell of all Your wondrous works.

PSALM 26:7 NKJV

LORD my God, I will praise you forever.

PSALM 30:12 NIV

And whatever you do, whether in word or deed,
do it all in the name of the Lord Jesus,
giving thanks to God the Father through him.

COLOSSIANS 3:17 NIV

Give thanks to the LORD, for he is good,
for his steadfast love endures forever.

PSALM 136:1 ESV

Let us come before His presence with thanksgiving;
let us shout joyfully to Him with psalms.

PSALM 95:2 NKJV

You are my God, and I will give thanks
to you; you are my God; I will extol you.
Oh give thanks to the LORD, for he is good;
for his steadfast love endures forever!

PSALM 118:28–29 ESV

"Blessing and glory and wisdom, thanksgiving
and honor and power and might, be to
our God forever and ever. Amen."

REVELATION 7:12 NKJV

"Bring me out of prison so I can thank you. The godly
will crowd around me for you are good to me."

PSALM 142:7 NLT

Make Much of the Little Things

Give thanks to the LORD, for he is good;
his love endures forever.

PSALM 107:1 NIV

Do you regularly count your blessings—the beauty and variety of wildflowers, the immensity of the evening sky, the power of the ocean's waves, the majestic heights of a mountain? Even when you forget to say thank you, God surrounds you with these things every day. Name three things in creation you take pleasure in, and give thanks to God for each of them. Your God made them for you simply because He wanted you to enjoy them.

Lord, break me free from my own prison when the challenges of life try to pin me in. Let my grateful heart cut me loose from the negative circumstances that weigh me down. Grateful praise silences the enemy, takes my mind off my problems, and shifts my thoughts onto You. Bring to my remembrance the many wonderful things You've placed in my life that I should be thankful for. I speak them aloud now.

Yes, but remember—those branches were broken off because they didn't believe in Christ, and you are there because you do believe. So don't think highly of yourself, but fear what could happen.

ROMANS 11:20 NLT

You have turned for me my mourning into dancing; You have put off my sackcloth and clothed me with gladness, to the end that my glory may sing praise to You and not be silent. O LORD my God, I will give thanks to You forever.

PSALM 30:11–12 NKJV

"We can always find something to be thankful for, and there may be reasons why we ought to be thankful for even those dispensations which appear dark and frowning."
ALBERT BARNES

"As we express our gratitude, we must never forget that the highest appreciation is not to utter words, but to live by them."
JOHN F. KENNEDY

"If you concentrate on finding whatever is good in every situation, you will discover that your life will suddenly be filled with gratitude, a feeling that nurtures the soul."
RABBI HAROLD KUSHNER

Sing to the LORD with grateful praise;
make music to our God on the harp.
PSALM 147:7 NIV

Therefore let us be grateful for receiving a
kingdom that cannot be shaken, and thus let us
offer to God acceptable worship, with reverence
and awe, for our God is a consuming fire.
HEBREWS 12:28–29 ESV

"But I, with shouts of grateful praise, will sacrifice
to you. What I have vowed I will make good.
I will say, 'Salvation comes from the LORD.' "
JONAH 2:9 NIV

Expectations

Looking Forward
While Looking Back

*Have you not known? Have you not heard? The LORD is
the everlasting God, the Creator of the ends of the earth.
He does not faint or grow weary; his understanding is
unsearchable. He gives power to the faint, and to him
who has no might he increases strength.*

ISAIAH 40:28–29 ESV

———

Susan tapped the side of her coffee mug with her long
fingernails. She did it unconsciously when she was
nervous. Her friend, Karyn, reach across the table and
touched her hand softly. "It's going to be okay," she said
encouragingly.

"I want to believe that," Susan replied, with worry
etched into her forehead, "but I don't want to get my
hopes up." Susan picked up Karyn's coffee cup and took
it to her kitchen for a refill. Returning to the table, she
continued: "As I look back over my life, I expected one

thing and it almost never turned out the way I imagined. You know I struggle when things are out of my control."

"Okay," Karyn said, "how many times have you cried out to God, felt like He wasn't there, only to discover He was working it out all along?"

Suddenly, Susan sensed God's presence, and a calm assurance comforted her. "God is here," she told Karyn. "It's like He's reminding me He's walked with me through it all before, and He's with me now."

"You can expect it all to work out for your best," Karyn said. "Sit back and let Him work out the details."

Surely there is a future,
and your hope will not be cut off.
PROVERBS 23:18 ESV

When you came down long ago, you did awesome
deeds beyond our highest expectations.
And oh, how the mountains quaked!
ISAIAH 64:3 NLT

For all creation is waiting eagerly for that future
day when God will reveal who his children really
are. Against its will, all creation was subjected
to God's curse. But with eager hope, the creation
looks forward to the day when it will join God's
children in glorious freedom from death and decay.
ROMANS 8:19–21 NLT

"I said to de Lord, 'I'm goin' to hold steady
on to you, an' I know you'll see me through."
HARRIET TUBMAN

"It's not what you look at that matters,
it's what you see."
HENRY DAVID THOREAU

"We are made wise not by the recollection of
our past, but by the responsibility for our future."
GEORGE BERNARD SHAW

"Obstacles are those frightful things you
see when you take your eyes off your goal."
HENRY FORD

He Never Fails

My soul, wait silently for God alone,
for my expectation is from Him.

PSALM 62:5 NKJV

Sometimes people fail to live up to your
expectations, and sometimes you fail to live up to
the values and standards you have for yourself.
As you take your hurt, your embarrassment, your
shame to God, don't forget His unchangeable love
for you. He has promised you the gift of His Holy
Spirit to give you strength and comfort, and you
should expect no less. He will never fail you.

Lord, each challenge I face is an opportunity to grow in my faith. Instead of making plans and plotting courses that lead to disappointment, give me wisdom and strength to believe that You are at work on my behalf. Whatever the circumstance, I hear Your voice and follow You. I release control to You and let You lead. Show me the way, Lord, as I step out behind You in faith.

*Whatever is good and perfect is a gift
coming down to us from God our Father,
who created all the lights in the heavens.
He never changes or casts a shifting shadow.*

JAMES 1:17 NLT

---

*The LORD has done it this very day;
let us rejoice today and be glad.*

PSALM 118:24 NIV

---

*And now, O Lord GOD, you are God, and your
words are true, and you have promised
this good thing to your servant.*

2 SAMUEL 7:28 ESV

---

*I open my mouth and pant, because I
long for your commandments.*

PSALM 119:131 ESV

*"Expect great things from God,
attempt great things for God."*
WILLIAM CAREY

———————

*"If he have faith, the believer cannot be
restrained. He betrays himself. He breaks out.
He confesses and teaches this gospel to
the people at the risk of life itself."*
MARTIN LUTHER

———————

*"People look to time in expectation that it will
eventually make them happy, but you cannot find
true happiness by looking toward the future."*
ECKHART TOLLE

———————

*"However many blessings we expect from God,
His infinite liberality will always exceed
all our wishes and our thoughts."*
JOHN CALVIN

Trust Him without Hesitation

In the morning, LORD, you hear my voice;
in the morning I lay my requests before
you and wait expectantly.
PSALM 5:3 NIV

You have taken your heartfelt requests to God,
and now you are waiting for His response. Don't
grow impatient. Instead, relish this time of hopeful
expectation. Rehearse the ways God has come
through for you in the past. Allow thanksgiving to
flow freely from your lips. Like a child on the day
before her birthday, enjoy a confident excitement
concerning what God is going to do on your behalf.
He is a gracious Father who can be trusted without
hesitation.

Heavenly Father, I make my requests known to You by faith. I believe that You know my heart and You direct my path. When I am disappointed because things don't happen as fast as I want or they look differently than I imagined, comfort me. Remind me that You have my very best interest at heart. Thank You, Lord, that no matter what happens, You work all things together for my good.

For I fully expect and hope that I will never be ashamed, but that I will continue to be bold for Christ, as I have been in the past. And I trust that my life will bring honor to Christ, whether I live or die.
PHILIPPIANS 1:20 NLT

———————————

And God is able to make all grace abound toward you, that you, always having all sufficiency in all things, may have an abundance for every good work.
2 CORINTHIANS 9:8 NKJV

Desires

More Like God

*Imitate God, therefore, in everything you do, because
you are his dear children. Live a life filled with love,
following the example of Christ. He loved us and offered
himself as a sacrifice for us, a pleasing aroma to God.*
Ephesians 5:1–2 nlt

Hannah and Rachel worked together packing groceries
for the food pantry their church hosted weekly for the
community. It was one of the few times each month they
could connect without their young children interrupting
their conversation. "So, how do you know for sure if a
desire is your own, or if it's a desire God put in your
heart?" Hannah asked Rachel.

"Like what?" Rachel replied.

"Well, like having another child, going back to
school, volunteering here each month together," Hannah
said. "I mean, it's easy to know bad desires that hurt us
or our relationship with God are not from Him."

Rachel stopped what she was doing and looked at her friend. "That's a great question. I guess for me, I have to stop and think about it. There's a scripture that says we are supposed to imitate God—so our desires should be reflective of His nature. If our desires are selfish and could bring harm or hurt to others, then it's probably not something God put in us."

Hannah gave her a high-five. "That's a great way to explain it. It makes so much sense. And when we choose those things that look like Him, we can let His peace guide us, as we pursue those desires from Him."

*Whom have I in heaven but you? And there is
nothing on earth that I desire besides you.
My flesh and my heart may fail, but God is the
strength of my heart and my portion forever.*

PSALM 73:25–26 ESV

---

*As the deer longs for streams of water, so I long
for you, O God. I thirst for God, the living God.
When can I go and stand before him?*

PSALM 42:1–2 NLT

---

*Let them praise the LORD for his great love
and for the wonderful things he has done
for them. For he satisfies the thirsty and
fills the hungry with good things.*

PSALM 107:8–9 NLT

"This desire for heart purity is a creation of the Holy Spirit at work in the heart."
DUNCAN CAMPBELL

"Longing desire prayeth always, though the tongue be silent. If thou art ever longing, thou art ever praying."
AUGUSTINE

"I care not where I go, or how I live, or what I endure so that I may save souls. When I sleep I dream of them; when I awake they are first in my thoughts no amount of scholastic attainment, of able and profound exposition of brilliant and stirring eloquence can atone for the absence of a deep impassioned sympathetic love for human souls."
DAVID BRAINERD

Heart Desires

*May He grant you according to your
heart's desire, and fulfill all your purpose.*
PSALM 20:4 NKJV

What is it you want with all your heart—true love,
a great job, children? Only you know what it is. You
needn't hold back. Because you are His child, He
longs to give you the things that would make you
happy. There are some conditions, though. Like any
good parent, He balances what you want with what
He knows is good for you. He isn't interested in
your temporary, superficial happiness. He wants to
give you more than you ever imagined.

Father, may the desires of my heart be pleasing to You. Teach me to recognize when my motives become selfish, self-serving, or displeasing to You. Give me a heart full of all that reflects Your image and truth. Fill me with Your presence. When others see me, may they see that what drives me more than anything else is a desire to please You and point others to relationship with You.

"People do not live by bread alone, but by every word that comes from the mouth of God."

MATTHEW 4:4 NLT

One thing I ask from the LORD, this only do I seek: that I may dwell in the house of the LORD all the days of my life, to gaze upon the beauty of the LORD and to seek him in his temple. My heart says of you, "Seek his face!" Your face, LORD, I will seek.

PSALM 27:4, 8 NIV

"My food," said Jesus, "is to do the will of him who sent me and to finish his work."

JOHN 4:34 NIV

"Christianity is not a theory or speculation, but a life; not a philosophy of life, but a living presence."
SAMUEL TAYLOR COLERIDGE

"Christianity provides a unified answer for the whole of life."
WILLIAM HENRY SEWARD

"To worship God in truth is further to admit that we are entirely contrary to Him, and that He is willing to make us like Himself if we desire it. Who will be so imprudent as to turn himself away, even for a moment, from the reverence, love, service and continual adoration which we most justly owe Him?"
BROTHER LAWRENCE

Longings of the Heart

Take delight in the LORD and he will
give you the desires of your heart.
Psalm 37:4 niv

As you get to know God better, as you bask in His
love and care, your desires will change. Selfishness
and unwholesome desires will fade away. You will
begin to understand and desire those things He
desires for you—those things that will resonate
in your heart and bring you true happiness. God
created you, and He knows you better than you
know yourself. Trust Him to give you the desires of
your heart.

Lord, Your Word speaks life to my circumstances and helps me to know and understand You more and more. Fill me with a desire to really comprehend what You are saying to me in the Bible. Give me a hunger to spend time getting to know You more as I study Your Word. May it illuminate my heart and mind and bring me a desire to grow intimately closer to You.

So get rid of all evil behavior. Be done with all deceit, hypocrisy, jealousy, and all unkind speech. Like newborn babies, you must crave pure spiritual milk so that you will grow into a full experience of salvation. Cry out for this nourishment.

1 PETER 2:1–2 NLT

The preparations of the heart belong to man, but the answer of the tongue is from the LORD. All the ways of a man are pure in his own eyes, but the LORD weighs the spirits. Commit your works to the LORD, and your thoughts will be established.

PROVERBS 16:1–3 NKJV

Beauty

Beauty's Mark

*But let your adorning be the hidden person of the heart
with the imperishable beauty of a gentle and quiet spirit,
which in God's sight is very precious.*

1 PETER 3:4 ESV

"People still stare," Elise said to her friend, Janna, as they sat down for lunch in the food court at the crowded mall they frequented. "It's been ten years and seven surgeries," she continued. "I know I'm never going to be the same, and people will always look at me differently."

Janna smiled knowingly at Elise. "I can never understand all that you've been through after the accident, but I do know that when I look at you, all I see is beauty. You are encouraging, inspiring, and committed to God and those who love you. You understand people in a way I've never experienced. You are perfect in my eyes, and I love you."

Elise's eyes filled with tears. "Most days I'm okay.

I don't think about how I look to others as much, but sometimes I let the peering eyes and pointing fingers get to me. Thank you!"

"I know those who love you, like I do, tell you this, but it's really true. You are marked with beauty. When people know you, they see the beautiful person that you are inside and out. I don't see the flaws or scars; I see my friend who reflects the heart of God. You are marked with His beauty, and even those who don't know you well are touched by Him through you."

He has made everything beautiful in its time.
He has also set eternity in the human heart;
yet no one can fathom what God has
done from beginning to end.
ECCLESIASTES 3:11 NIV

Charm is deceitful, and beauty is vain,
but a woman who fears the LORD is to be praised.
PROVERBS 31:30 ESV

"Look beneath the surface
so you can judge correctly."
JOHN 7:24 NLT

For you are all children of the light and of the day;
we don't belong to darkness and night.
1 THESSALONIANS 5:5 NLT

"Never lose an opportunity for
seeing anything that is beautiful;
For beauty is God's handwriting–
a wayside sacrament.
Welcome it in every fair face,
in every fair sky, in every fair flower,
And thank God for it as a cup of His blessing."
RALPH WALDO EMERSON

"Beauty is but the sensible image of the Infinite.
Like truth and justice it lives within us; like virtue
and the moral law it is a companion of the soul."
CHARLES W. H. BANCROFT

"The beauty of a woman must be seen from in her
eyes, because that is the doorway to her heart,
the place where love resides."
AUDREY HEPBURN

Beauty Within

Don't be concerned about the outward beauty of fancy hairstyles, expensive jewelry, or beautiful clothes. You should clothe yourselves instead with the beauty that comes from within, the unfading beauty of a gentle and quiet spirit, which is so precious to God.

1 PETER 3:3–4 NLT

Twenty-first-century women are exposed to an almost impossible standard of beauty. And the message is unrelenting. In such an environment, every little flaw or blemish can be devastating. God says that outward beauty is of no consequence unless there is beauty on the inside. After all, even the most beautiful woman cannot hope to keep her looks for long. The beautiful, godly soul, however, lives forever.

Lord, this world is all about image, but thankfully I am not of this world—I just have to live in it. When I struggle to feel valued by others because of how I look, or don't look, help me to remember that my worth doesn't come from others. Their definition of beauty is not Your definition. Help me to recognize beauty by Your definition in myself and in others today.

And he gives grace generously.
As the Scriptures say, "God opposes the
proud but gives grace to the humble."
JAMES 4:6 NLT

You are altogether beautiful,
my love; there is no flaw in you.
SONG OF SOLOMON 4:7 ESV

The LORD will hold you in his hand for all to see—
a splendid crown in the hand of God.
ISAIAH 62:3 NLT

"The best part of beauty is that which no picture can express."
FRANCIS BACON

"Beauty is in the heart of the beholder."
H. G. WELLS

"If you get simple beauty and naught else, you get about the best thing God invents."
ROBERT BROWNING

"I don't think of all the misery but of the beauty that still remains."
ANNE FRANK

You're a Divine Work of Art

"The LORD does not look at the things people look at. People look at the outward appearance, but the LORD looks at the heart."

1 SAMUEL 16:7 NIV

Who says what is beautiful and what is not? It would seem that the creator of a work of art would be the one whose opinion matters most. For the creator, every nuance, every brushstroke, every indention in the clay has meaning. God created you—with intention and purpose. You are His work of art. In His eyes, you are beautiful in every way, inside and out.

Heavenly Father, thank You for making me perfect in Your sight. Others do not see what You see in me. When I am tempted to feel less than who I am and cave to the judgements of who the world says I am, remind me of what You see in me. I am Your masterpiece. May I become the work of art You desire me to be.

Then God said, "Let us make man in our image, after our likeness. And let them have dominion over the fish of the sea and over the birds of the heavens and over the livestock and over all the earth and over every creeping thing that creeps on the earth." So God created man in his own image, in the image of God he created him; male and female he created them.

GENESIS 1:26–27 ESV

But you are to be perfect, even as your Father in heaven is perfect.

MATTHEW 5:48 NLT

Christ is the visible image of the invisible God. He existed before anything was created and is supreme over all creation.

COLOSSIANS 1:15 NLT

Adversity

In Difficult Times

He brought me out into a broad place;
he rescued me, because he delighted in me.
PSALM 18:19 ESV

———————————

"Every idea, every plan I have just crumbles," Gina complained to her mother, Rosalyn. "I have never struggled like this in my life. It seems like almost every door I knock on is locked, and when I find one slightly open, I push a little and realize the chain is on the door, and then it eventually slams in my face."

Rosalyn smiled at her daughter as they chatted on Facetime. "I'm sorry this is such a difficult season. Moving to a new place and trying to find a place to live, start a new job, and make new friends is a lot to take on. But you're an overcomer, and He is your comfort in the hard times."

"That's easy for you to say," Gina mumbled.

Rosalyn's voice sharpened. "Gina, has He ever failed you?"

Her mother's words pricked her heart. "No," Gina admitted. "But it's so hard to wait on Him to bring me through."

"Then take your eyes off your troubles, and allow Him to comfort you as you remember all the things He's done for you."

Gina said good-bye to her mom and put down her phone. She began to remember some of the special things God had done. She began to recite each one and thank Him. His faithfulness comforted her. She knew she would make it through.

Search me, God, and know my heart;
test me and know my anxious thoughts.

PSALM 139:23 NIV

So we do not lose heart. Though our outer self
is wasting away, our inner self is being renewed
day by day. For this light momentary affliction is
preparing for us an eternal weight of glory beyond
all comparison, as we look not to the things that
are seen but to the things that are unseen. For
the things that are seen are transient, but the
things that are unseen are eternal.

2 CORINTHIANS 4:16–18 ESV

"I am still determined to be cheerful and happy, in whatever situation I may be; for I have also learned from experience that the greater part of our happiness or misery depends upon our dispositions, and not upon our circumstances."

MARTHA WASHINGTON

"Trials teach us what we are; they dig up the soil, and let us see what we are made of; they just turn up some of the ill weeds onto the surface."

CHARLES SPURGEON

"As for courage and will—we cannot measure how much of each lies within us, we can only trust there will be sufficient to carry through trials which may lie ahead."

OVID

He Has Your Answer

"Do not fear or be dismayed: tomorrow go out against them for the LORD is with you."

2 CHRONICLES 20:17 NKJV

Adversity, calamity, hardship, misfortune, trouble, hard times—no matter what you call them, these painful episodes are part of the human experience. But you can choose to not let them bring you down, fill you with fear, and steal your attention from the blessings God has placed in your life. Look adversity square in the eye and know that your God—the God of all comfort—has an answer.

God, You know every hardship I'll ever face. You know exactly what I'm going through right now. I need Your peace and strength to travel this difficult road. I trust in Your promises. No matter what I face, You are with me. You will bring me out of the darkness and into the light. You will turn my mourning into dancing and my sorrow into joy. Comfort me with Your presence, and assure me with Your love today.

"This is my command—be strong and courageous!
Do not be afraid or discouraged. For the LORD
your God is with you wherever you go."
JOSHUA 1:9 NLT

———————————

Give thanks in all circumstances;
for this is God's will for you in Christ Jesus.
1 THESSALONIANS 5:18 NIV

———————————

We are hard pressed on every side, yet not crushed;
we are perplexed, but not in despair; persecuted,
but not forsaken; struck down, but not destroyed.
2 CORINTHIANS 4:8–9 NKJV

———————————

Dear brothers and sisters, when troubles of any kind
come your way, consider it an opportunity for great
joy. For you know that when your faith is tested,
your endurance has a chance to grow.
JAMES 1:2–3 NLT

*"Thou my everlasting portion,
More than friend or life to me,
All along my pilgrim journey,
Savior, let me walk with Thee."*
FANNY J. CROSBY

---

*"O what a blessed day that will be when I shall . . . look
back on the raging seas I have safely passed; when I
shall review my pains and sorrows, my fears and tears,
and possess the glory which was the end of all!"*
RICHARD BAXTER

"Earth has no sorrow that heaven cannot heal."
THOMAS MOORE

Your Friend in Adversity

A friend loves at all times,
and a brother is born for adversity.
PROVERBS 17:17 NKJV

When you give your heart and life to God, the Bible says Jesus Christ becomes your friend and your brother—and that changes everything. You aren't alone when adversity strikes. You've become a member of God's family and part of His circle of friends. His resources are marshaled in your defense, and His loving Holy Spirit—the Bible calls Him the Comforter—is with you constantly.

Lord, when life brings hurt and pain, I will remember that I am not alone. You have been through adversity. You suffered through and understand all the hardships I will ever face. Knowing You understand, I don't have to do this alone. I come to You and pour out my heart. You know what I am feeling. I draw comfort from You. With You by my side, I will get through this storm.

For he will hide me in his shelter in the day of trouble; he will conceal me under the cover of his tent; he will lift me high upon a rock. And now my head shall be lifted up above my enemies all around me, and I will offer in his tent sacrifices with shouts of joy; I will sing and make melody to the LORD.

PSALM 27:5–6 ESV

———————————————

Rejoice in our confident hope.
Be patient in trouble, and keep on praying.

ROMANS 12:12 NLT

Healing

Tears of Healing

The eyes of the LORD are on the righteous,
and His ears are open to their cry.
PSALM 34:15 NKJV

Monica turned up the speakers on her phone as she began her long commute home. She recognized the next song on the playlist, and she knew the words would soothe her aching heart. She took a deep breath and tried to relax. She deliberately loosened her grip on the steering wheel. She felt the lump rising in her throat. This time she refused to repress it, instead she chose to embrace it and let it go.

As the familiar words began, she felt Jesus beside her and knew it was okay to let it all go. She welcomed the wet, hot tears as they slid down her face. She felt the Lord's comfort and assurance.

It didn't matter that she couldn't sing the words. The artist's lyrics spoke what she felt. Besides, she couldn't get a word out if she wanted to. Instead, she opened her heart wide and let the presence of God pour over her. With each verse of the song she felt herself letting go—slowly—of the pain and hurt.

As the last of the song played, she felt a peace. The tears she shed washed through her and released the final hurts from the deepest part of her heart. She knew the Lord was at work, carefully and deliberately healing her soul.

You keep track of all my sorrows. You have collected all my tears in your bottle.
You have recorded each one in your book.

PSALM 56:8 NLT

———————————

But he was pierced for our transgressions;
he was crushed for our iniquities; upon him
was the chastisement that brought us peace,
and with his wounds we are healed.

ISAIAH 53:5 ESV

———————————

The thief does not come except to steal, and to kill,
and to destroy. I have come that they may have life,
and that they may have it more abundantly.

JOHN 10:10 NKJV

"Let your tears come. Let them water your soul."
ELEEN MAYHEW

"Heaven knows we need never be ashamed of
our tears, for they are rain upon the blinding
dust of earth, overlying our hard hearts."
CHARLES DICKENS

"The Christian life is not a constant high. I have
my moments of deep discouragement. I have
to go to God in prayer with tears in my eyes,
and say, 'O God, forgive me,' or 'Help me.'"
BILLY GRAHAM

Soul Healer

[God] heals the brokenhearted
and binds up their wounds.
PSALM 147:3 NIV

_____

God has promised to see you through the
most painful hours of your life, but His love and
compassion don't end there. If you let Him, He will
pick up the pieces of your broken heart and put
them back together again. Your tears are precious
to your heavenly Father, your suffering never
wasted. You can trust Him to understand your
sorrow—even enter into it with you—as He brings
healing and new life from the ashes.

Heavenly Father, this life is filled with ups and downs. I know I live in a fallen world and life brings hurts and sorrow. When my heart is overwhelmed, help me to use my emotions in a positive way that brings healing to my life and the lives around me. Remind me to walk close to You and trust You to heal every hurt of my soul.

*"He will wipe every tear from their eyes,
and there will be no more death or
sorrow or crying or pain. All these
things are gone forever."*
REVELATION 21:4 NLT

---

*When the righteous cry for help, the LORD hears and
delivers them out of all their troubles. The LORD is
near to the brokenhearted and saves the crushed
in spirit. Many are the afflictions of the righteous,
but the LORD delivers him out of them all. He keeps
all his bones; not one of them is broken.*
PSALM 34:17–20 ESV

"There is a sacredness in tears. They are not the mark of weakness, but of power. They speak more eloquently than ten thousand tongues. They are the messengers of overwhelming grief, of deep contrition, and of unspeakable love."

WASHINGTON IRVING

"Christ always preached doctrine that was hopeful. While he denounced self-righteousness, he would turn round and say, 'I came not to call the righteous, but sinners to repentance.' If he ever had a frown on his brow, it was for the hypocrite and the proud man. But he had tears for sinners and loving invitations for penitent ones."

CHARLES SPURGEON

Hope in the Dark

The LORD is close to the brokenhearted
and saves those who are crushed in spirit.

PSALM 34:18 NIV

God's love is manifest at all times in our lives, but
never so much as when our hearts are breaking.
It is then that we experience His compassion and
comfort in ways we cannot even imagine during
the good times. When you've suffered a betrayal,
loss or disappointment, when life threatens to bury
you under the cold, hard ground, God is there with
hope and comfort in your darkest hour.

Lord, when I am disappointed and hurt, You are my comfort. When I experience loss or betrayal, You feel my pain. Give me wisdom to use my emotions in a way that promotes healing. Help me to share my grief with You and with others I can trust. Give me courage to do the difficult things I need to do as a result of my pain. Show me how to process it all with hope and healing from You.

While Jesus was here on earth, he offered prayers and pleadings, with a loud cry and tears, to the one who could rescue him from death. And God heard his prayers because of his deep reverence for God.

HEBREWS 5:7 NLT

In my distress I called upon the LORD, and cried out to my God; He heard my voice from His temple, and my cry came before Him, even to His ears.

PSALM 18:6 NKJV

Those who sow in tears shall reap with shouts of joy!

PSALM 126:5 ESV

Strength

In His Presence Is Strength

My soul will be satisfied as with fat and rich food, and my mouth will praise you with joyful lips, when I remember you upon my bed, and meditate on you in the watches of the night; for you have been my help, and in the shadow of your wings I will sing for joy. My soul clings to you; your right hand upholds me.

PSALM 63:5–8 ESV

Most Friday mornings, a little before 5 a.m., Lyla almost skipped through the doors of the neonatal intensive-care unit, but today she was numb. As a volunteer she enjoyed cuddling those little babies and helping out in whatever way was needed.

Sierra, one of the nurses, immediately noticed Lyla's low spirits. "Where's your joyful bounce today?" she teased.

Lyla smiled a half smile. "It's been a rough week."

Sierra could tell she didn't want to elaborate so patted her gently on the back. Lyla slipped into one of the rooms with a crying baby, changed his diaper and swaddled him. She took him into her arms and sat down in one of the rocking chairs.

Her heart hurt and tears slid silently down her cheeks. She'd really told no one but God about the situation. She looked down at the sweet little face nestled into her arms. As she rocked him, the pain in her heart began to subside. With the back and forth motion of the rocking chair, she allowed her Savior to fill her with His strength.

"May the Holy Spirit be my personal guide always so that I will live only for Him. May I overflow in love so as to draw others to Christ and may His strength be perfected in my weakness."
CAMERON TOWNSEND

"Deny your weakness, and you will never realize God's strength in you."
JONI EARECKSON TADA

"Do not strive in your own strength; cast yourself at the feet of the Lord Jesus, and wait upon Him in the sure confidence that He is with you, and works in you. Strive in prayer; let faith fill your heart—so will you be strong in the Lord, and in the power of His might."
ANDREW MURRAY

God, sometimes I get so tired in the crazy battle. There are so many obstacles I've faced, and I didn't have to face any of them alone. I can make it because You are with me. You've promised never to leave me. Time spent in Your presence gives me everything I need to press on. It's not up to me and my ability. I can do all things in Your strength.

As soon as I pray, you answer me;
you encourage me by giving me strength.

PSALM 138:3 NLT

This is my command—be strong and courageous!
Do not be afraid or discouraged. For the LORD
your God is with you wherever you go.

JOSHUA 1:9 NLT

God is our refuge and strength,
always ready to help in times of trouble.

PSALM 46:1 NLT

If I ride the wings of the morning, if I dwell by
the farthest oceans, even there your hand will
guide me, and your strength will support me.

PSALM 139:9–10 NLT

*"Worry does not empty tomorrow of its sorrows;
it empties today of its strength."*
CORRIE TEN BOOM

---

*"Faith is often strengthened right
at the place of disappointment."*
RODNEY MCBRIDE

---

*"If we go forth in our own strength, we shall faint,
and utterly fall; but having our hearts and our
hopes in heaven, we shall be carried above all
difficulties, and be enabled to lay hold of the
prize of our high calling in Christ Jesus."*
MATTHEW HENRY

Strength That's Not Your Own

The Lord is faithful, and he will strengthen and protect you from the evil one.

2 THESSALONIANS 3:3 NIV

God never expects you to hold on to your faith by your own strength. He knows the weakness of all human hearts, and He knows all about the temptations you deal with every day. With His own strength, God will defend you! Ask the Holy Spirit to give you His strength and power, so you will exercise your spiritual muscles and move beyond your frailty. Where you are weak, God is strong.

Lord, when I am weak, You are my strength. I refuse to believe the lie that I have to make things happen in my own strength. It's not up to me—it's up to You. You are my strong tower. You are my fortress. Fill me with Your strength and power. Help me to work to build my faith and grow in my trust in You.

"Fear not, for I have redeemed you; I have called you by name, you are mine. When you pass through the waters, I will be with you; and through the rivers, they shall not overwhelm you; when you walk through fire you shall not be burned, and the flame shall not consume you. For I am the LORD your God, the Holy One of Israel, your Savior.

ISAIAH 43:1–3 ESV

———————————

The LORD is my strength and song, and He has become my salvation; He is my God, and I will praise Him; my father's God, and I will exalt Him.

EXODUS 15:2 NKJV